# Checkers Cookery Collection

# SHORT-CUT COOKING

## Checkers

**Written and recipes developed by Norma MacMillan**

Published exclusively for Checkers Stores
by Cathay Books, 59 Grosvenor Street, London W1

First published 1986

© Cathay Books 1986

ISBN 0 86178 391 3

Printed in Hong Kong

## ACKNOWLEDGEMENTS

The publishers would like to thank the following companies
for their kindness in providing materials and equipment
used in the photography for this book.

David Mellor, 4 Sloane Square, London SW1

World's End Tiles, 9 Langton Street, London SW1


We would also like to thank the following
who were concerned in the preparation of the book.

*Series Art Director* Pedro Prá-Lopez

*Photographer* Trevor Richards

*Stylist* Sue Russell

*Food prepared for photography by* Judy Bugg

*Special editorial help* Cathy Dunn

# CONTENTS

**NOTE**

Standard spoon measurements are used in all recipes

1 tablespoon (tbls) = one 15 ml spoon
1 teaspoon (tsp) = one 5 ml spoon
All spoon measures are level

All eggs are sized 3 or 4 (standard) unless otherwise stated.

For all recipes, quantities are given in both metric and imperial
measures. Follow either set but not a mixture of both, as they are
not interchangeable.

$A$s South Africa's largest supermarket chain, we are pledged to giving you, our customer, a hassle-free shopping trip. This was why we set up Consumer Centres in stores and appointed Customer Care Managers in the larger supermarkets.

The tremendous success of this service and the continued requests for more recipes and information has now prompted us to obtain for you our own special range of Checkers Cookery Books.

Our series started with 12 books and following the success of these, we are delighted to be adding 7 new titles to the series. Each book contains practical background information on the chosen subject and concentrates on a wide selection of carefully tested recipes, each one illustrated in colour.

*Short-Cut Cooking* offers a repertoire of impressive but easy-to-prepare dishes for the busy or reluctant cook. We offer tips on how to transform ready prepared foods or delicatessen goods into creative dishes for that instant occasion, as well as recipes that are prepared from scratch using short-cut and time saving methods. The recipes cover a wide variety of hot and cold starters, main courses and puddings as well as special menu recipes for impromptu entertaining. Whatever the occasion, you can be confident you'll have more time to enjoy it – and your meal – with the help of this book.

I very much hope you will enjoy looking through *Short-Cut Cooking* and trying the recipes.

Happy, relaxed cooking!

Clive Weil, Managing Director, Checkers S.A. Ltd.

# *INTRODUCTION*

This is a book specially written for busy people. If you are on the go all day – working in an office, shop or factory, or at home – the last thing you want to do is spend hours in the kitchen preparing an evening meal. You may have other activities planned – a favourite sport, a visit to the cinema or theatre, or even just relaxing with a book or in front of the television.

There are occasions, too, when you want to entertain your friends and family, but don't have the time or inclination to devote hours to cooking.

The recipes that follow employ simple short-cuts to save time in preparation and cooking, but the results are still delicious.

By using the aptly named 'convenience' foods and delicatessen goods in an imaginative way, dishes can be prepared more quickly, with less effort on the part of the cook.

A well-stocked store cupboard is a vital part of short-cut cooking. By adding fresh or frozen ingredients to canned or packaged foods, interesting dishes can be prepared very easily and quickly.

Useful canned foods to have readily at hand are: canned condensed soups such as cream of tomato, cream of mushroom and cream of chicken; canned fish and shellfish such as tuna, salmon, crab, shrimps, sardines, anchovies and so on – are useful substitutes for fresh fish, but also good for garnishes and sauces in other dishes; canned beans such as red kidney, cannellini, flageolet and chick peas; canned vegetables such as tomatoes, sweetcorn, carrots and potatoes; canned corned beef; and canned fruits in natural juice such as pineapple, peaches, mandarin oranges, pears and apricots.

Dry packaged soups, pudding mixes and sauces as well as packets of fruit jellies are also excellent standbys. Dried pasta in various shapes and sizes is always worth stocking for several reasons. For its nutritional value, its versatility and speed of cooking. Bottled salad dressings, mayonnaise, jams and pickled vegetables have their place in the store cupboard, too.

Delicatessen cooked meats and smoked fish can be the main ingredient in short-cut savoury dishes, and purchased cakes, sponge flan or pastry cases and meringue nests are wonderful bases for extra quick desserts.

Another excellent short-cut in the kitchen is to use time-saving equipment. Electric blenders, mixers and food processors are a boon to a busy cook, and can make light work of the laborious sieving, mashing, chopping and whisking that once had to be done by hand.

The recipes in the main part of this book are divided into first courses, main courses and puddings; they can be mixed to form two- and three-course meals according to the occasion and your taste. To help you on your way, we have provided a week's menu planning (p. 6). The last chapter is devoted to short-cut entertaining and provides you with a selection of special menus which will impress your guests and leave you time to enjoy their company!

Finally, in each of these four chapters we have also given you some extra short-cut tips – quick recipe ideas that add a special touch and save you time and effort as well.

# Menu planning for everyday

For everyday meals, here are some suggestions for a week's
evening meal menus, all using recipes in this book:

### MONDAY
Continental meat platter
(recipe tip p. 7)
Chef's salad (p. 40)
Butterscotch rice desserts
(p. 46)

### THURSDAY
Quick muffin pizzas (p. 19)
Steak with pepper cheese
(recipe tip p. 20)
Frozen cream moulds (p. 43)

### TUESDAY
Smoked cheese and apple
appetiser (p. 16)
Short cut shepherds pie
(recipe tip p. 20)
Hot fruit compôte
(recipe tip p. 42)

### FRIDAY
Hummus (p. 16)
Mango chicken (p. 36)
Creamy ginger cheesecakes
(p. 49)

### WEDNESDAY
Curried tuna pâté (p. 13)
Pizza frittata (p. 33)
Quick apple snow (recipe tip
p. 42)

### SATURDAY
Tomato soup (p. 8)
Seafood gratin (p. 24)
Peach and almond crumble
(p. 50)

### SUNDAY
Devilled chicken livers (p. 18)
Island pork chops (p. 32)
Apricot topped almond
shortbreads (p. 53)

# FIRST COURSES

The first course sets the style of a meal and balances and complements what is to follow. It should not be too heavy or rich if the main course is substantial, and it should not include the same ingredients as the main course. It's worth considering the colour and texture of different dishes, too; a contrast is very appealing.

A cold starter can usually be served before a hot main dish and is a help to the busy cook as it enables him or her to prepare the starter well in advance. But take account of the weather, also, when planning a menu – on cold days a warming soup will be welcoming, less so on a sultry summer's evening.

Interesting starters can be prepared very quickly with the clever use of convenience and delicatessen foods. Smoked and pickled fish such as rollmops are excellent in first courses, as are certain cheeses and cooked meats such as salamis, ham and thinly sliced smoked and cured meats like pork, turkey or chicken.

**Here are a few quick tips:**

– Assemble a Continental style platter of thinly sliced cooked meats (salami, ham, cervelat, mortadella sausage, etc.) and garnish it attractively with gherkins, pickled cocktail onions, olives and radishes. Serve with hot French bread and unsalted butter.
– Make a quick dip by gently melting 100-150 g (4-5 oz) grated Cheddar cheese with 4-6 tbls bottled taco sauce. Serve in a heatproof dish over a candle flame or spirit burner, with corn or taco chips for dipping.
– Wrap slices of prosciutto (parma ham) or honey-roast ham around wedges of ripe melon, mango, avocado or dessert pear.
– Mix 225 g (8 oz) full-fat soft cheese with 100 g (4 oz) pineapple or apricot preserves. Shape into a flat cake and coat with crushed walnuts or pecan nuts. Chill well before serving with cornish wafer biscuits.
– Brush water biscuits with melted butter or margarine and sprinkle over caraway, celery or sesame seeds. Bake at 180°C/350°F/Gas Mark 4 for 5 minutes. These can be eaten on their own or crushed and sprinkled over hot soup. Make a salad of shredded iceberg lettuce, crisply cooked chopped bacon and bottled french dressing, liberally sprinkle the crushed biscuits on top.
– Mix 2 tbls dried onion soup mix with 300 ml (½ pt) soured cream, or half soured cream and half natural yoghurt. If liked, fold in 50 g (2 oz) crumbled Danish blue cheese. Cover and chill for at least 2 hours before serving as a dip with crisps and raw vegetables, or as a salad dressing. This is also an excellent topping for baked jacket potatoes.
– Remove crusts from slices of bread, cut into fingers and toast them. Spread with butter or garlic- and herb-flavoured soft cheese and arrange drained canned asparagus spears on top. Cover with slices of cheese and grill until the cheese has melted. Sprinkle with either cayenne pepper or paprika and serve the asparagus toasts hot.
– Heat 1 × 425 g (15 oz) can tomato soup with a little crushed dried rosemary, then stir in 2 tbls thawed frozen concentrated orange juice. Serve topped with natural yoghurt and chopped chives.

# Chilled carrot and orange soup

**SERVES** 4-6

*539 g (1 lb 3 oz) can carrots,*
  *drained*
*150 ml (¼ pint) orange juice*
*300 ml (½ pint) chicken stock,*
  *made from stock cube*
*salt and pepper*
**To garnish:**
*chopped fresh parsley, chives or*
  *dill*

Place the carrots, orange juice and stock in a blender or food processor and process until smooth. Add seasoning to taste.

Pour the soup into a jug or bowl and chill well.

To serve, pour the soup into individual cups, bowls or glasses and top each with a sprinkling of parsley, chives or dill.

# Bacon and bean soup

**SERVES** 4-6

*125 g (4 oz) unsmoked back bacon,*
  *trimmed and chopped*
*1 onion, finely chopped*
*1 garlic clove, crushed*
*1 small carrot, finely diced*
*1 tbls flour*
*600 ml (1 pint) chicken stock, made*
  *from a stock cube*
*300 ml (½ pint) skimmed milk*
*439 g (15½ oz) can red kidney*
  *beans, drained and rinsed*
*439 g (15½ oz) can butter beans,*
  *drained and rinsed*
*198 g (7 oz) can sweetcorn kernels,*
  *drained*
*2 tbls chopped fresh sage or 1 tsp*
  *dried sage*
*pepper to taste*
*grated cheese, to serve (optional)*

Sauté the bacon in a large saucepan for 1-2 minutes. Add the onion, garlic and carrot and cook, stirring occasionally, until the onion is softened. Add the flour and stir over the heat until absorbed by the fat. Add the stock and milk and bring to the boil. Simmer for 10 minutes, stirring occasionally.

Stir in the beans, sweetcorn, sage and pepper to taste. Simmer for a further 10 minutes. Serve hot with grated cheese, if using.

# Tomato soup

**SERVES** 4

*1 small onion, finely chopped*
*15 g (½ oz) butter*
*300 ml (½ pint) tomato juice*
*300 ml (½ pint) beef stock*
*400 g (14 oz) can chopped*
  *tomatoes*
*2 tsp sugar*
*½ tsp dried basil*
*1 bay leaf*
*salt and pepper*
**To serve:**
*4 tbls soured cream or Greek-style*
  *strained yoghurt*
*grated Parmesan cheese*

Cook the onion in the butter in a saucepan until soft but not browned. Add the tomato juice, stock, tomatoes with their juice, sugar, basil, bay leaf. Season to taste. Stir and bring to the boil.

Reduce the heat and simmer gently for 15 minutes. Stir occasionally.

Discard the bay leaf, and pour the soup into a blender or food processor. Blend until smooth. Alternatively, for a smoother result, rub the soup through a nylon sieve.

Reheat the soup, taste and adjust the seasoning. Ladle into soup bowls and top each serving with a spoonful of soured cream or yoghurt and a little Parmesan cheese.

● **Bacon and bean soup; Chilled carrot and orange soup; Tomato soup**

# Quick gravlax

**SERVES 4**

225 g (8 oz) smoked salmon, thinly
  sliced
dill sprigs, to garnish
**For the marinade:**
2 tbls olive oil
½ tbls red wine vinegar
½ tbls lemon juice
1 tbls brandy
1 tsp caster sugar
¼ tsp dry mustard
salt and pepper
1 tbls chopped fresh dill

Place all the marinade ingredients,
except for the chopped dill in a
screw-top jar and shake until well
blended. Add the chopped fresh dill
and shake again briefly.

Place one slice of salmon on a plate
and pour over a little of the dressing.
Rub the dressing into the salmon
using the fingertips, then turn the
fish over and repeat on the other
side. Continue 'dressing' each slice
of salmon, then roll each slice of
salmon and arrange on four individual serving plates.

Pour remaining dressing over the
salmon. Cover and marinate at room
temperature for 30 minutes.

Serve with brown bread and
garnish with dill sprigs.

# Smoked fish with goat's cheese sauce

**SERVES 4**

4 fillets of fish (buckling, mackerel,
  etc.)
1 orange, peeled and sliced
2 hard-boiled eggs, sliced
100 g (4 oz) crumbly goat's cheese,
  such as feta
4 tbls mayonnaise
4 tbls soured cream or natural
  yoghurt
1 egg white (optional)
sprig of rue, to garnish (optional)

Cut the fillets into small, bite-sized
pieces or leave whole if preferred and
arrange on four serving plates, with
the orange and egg slices.

Put goat's cheese, mayonnaise
and soured cream or yoghurt in a
blender or food processor and blend
until smooth. Alternatively, beat all
ingredients with a wooden spoon
until smooth. If a fluffy sauce is
preferred, beat the egg white until
stiff and fold it into the sauce.

Spoon the sauce onto the plates
and serve garnished with rue, if
using.

# Smoked fish pâté

**SERVES 4-6**

*4 fillets of mackerel, buckling or
   Arbroath smokies
75 g (3 oz) full fat soft cheese
1-2 tbls lemon juice
1-2 tbls creamed horseradish
pepper
lemon slices, to garnish*

Place the fish fillets in a blender or food processor and add the cheese. Blend until smooth. Add lemon juice, horseradish and pepper to taste and mix. For a coarser pâté, flake and mash fish with a fork, then beat in remaining ingredients.

Pack the pâté into a serving dish. Cover and chill for at least 2 hours. Garnish with the lemon slices.

**Serving idea:** Serve with squares of freshly made melba toast.

● Top: Smoked fish pâté; Bottom: Smoked fish with goat's cheese sauce; Quick gravlax

# Egg and caviar mould

**SERVES 4**

15 g (½ oz) sachet powdered
  gelatine
3 tbls water
2 hard-boiled eggs
5 tbls mayonnaise
5 tbls soured cream or natural
  yoghurt
3 tbls chopped fresh chives or
  1½ tbls dried chives
2 tbls chopped fresh parsley or
  1 tbls dried parsley
1 tsp Dijon mustard
1 tbls lemon juice
salt and pepper
**To serve:**
5 tbls soured cream or natural
  yoghurt
50 g (2 oz) black lumpfish caviar or
  shrimps

Sprinkle the gelatine over the water
in a small heatproof bowl. Leave for
2-3 minutes until spongy. Stand
bowl in a pan of hot water until the
gelatine has dissolved. Remove from
heat and cool slightly.

Place the eggs, mayonnaise,
soured cream or yoghurt, chives,
parsley, mustard, lemon juice and
seasoning to taste in a blender or
food processor. Blend until well
combined. (The mixture will not be
completely smooth.) Add the dissolved gelatine and blend again.

Pour into a 450 ml (¾ pint) capacity mould and chill in the refrigerator until set (about 3-4 hours).

When ready to serve, loosen the
egg mixture with a knife, then dip
the bottom of the mould briefly in
hot water. Turn out onto a serving
plate. Spoon over the soured cream
or yoghurt, letting it run down the
sides. Then spoon over the caviar or
shrimps.

***Serving idea:*** Serve with thin slices
of brown bread and butter.

● Below: Egg and caviar mould; Top right: Curried tuna pâté; Rollmops with apple
and beetroot

# Curried tuna pâté

**SERVES 4-6**

*198 g (7 oz) can tuna, drained*
*3 tbls mayonnaise*
*1 tsp Madras curry powder*
*1 tbls lemon juice*
*salt and pepper*
*1 dessert apple, peeled, cored and*
  *finely chopped*
*2 tbls chopped fresh chives*
**To garnish:**
*piece of lemon*
*sprigs of parsley*

Put the tuna into a blender or food processor and add the mayonnaise, curry powder, lemon juice and seasoning to taste. Blend until smooth. Beat in the other ingredients.

Add the apple and chives and fold into the pâté until well mixed.

Pack the pâté into a serving dish and chill. Garnish with lemon and parsley and serve with hot toast.

# Rollmops with apple and beetroot

**SERVES 4**

*1 large red-skinned apple, cored*
  *and thinly sliced*
*lemon juice*
*325 g (12 oz) jar rollmops with*
  *onions and gherkins, drained*
*150 g (5.29 oz) carton natural*
  *yoghurt*
*salt and pepper*
*2 hard-boiled eggs, sliced*
*4 pickled beetroot, sliced*

Toss the apple slices in lemon juice to prevent discoloration. Drain off excess juice.

Unroll the rollmops and cut into slices crossways. Place in a mixing bowl, with chopped onion and gherkins, and add the apple slices, yoghurt and seasoning to taste. Fold together gently.

Spoon the rollmop mixture onto individual serving plates and arrange egg slices on one side. Pat dry the beetroot slices with kitchen paper towels, then arrange them in a line or curve on the other side of the rollmop mixture.

# Salami and cheese cornets

**SERVES 6**

50 g (2 oz) Edam cheese, finely
  grated
2 tbls mayonnaise
3 sweet-sour pickled gherkins,
  diced
1 tsp creamed horseradish or
  horseradish sauce
12 thin slices salami or cervelat
  sausage
**To garnish:**
black olives
parsley sprigs

Combine the cheese, mayonnaise, gherkins and horseradish in a mixing bowl. Blend with a fork until the mixture holds together and is rather sticky.

Divide the cheese mixture between the salami slices, placing it just off centre. Fold over the sides of the slices to form cornet shapes and press together to seal. Chill slightly to keep in shape.

Arrange the cornets on a serving dish and garnish with black olives and parsley sprigs.

*Variation:* Use small pieces of salami to make an attractive dish for cocktail parties.

# Lobster and prawn mousse

**SERVES 6**

15 g (½ oz) sachet powdered
  gelatine
3 tbls water
425 g (15 oz) can lobster bisque
225 g (8 oz) full fat soft cheese,
2 tsp creamed horseradish
2 tbls chopped fresh parsley
1 tbls lemon juice
100 g (4 oz) cooked peeled prawns,
  thawed and drained if frozen
watercress, to garnish

Sprinkle gelatine over water in a small heatproof bowl and leave for 2-3 minutes until spongy. Stand bowl in a pan of hot water until gelatine dissolves. Remove from heat and cool slightly.

Place the soup, cheese, horseradish, parsley and lemon juice in a blender or food processor and blend until smooth. Taste and add more lemon juice if desired. Add gelatine and blend. Stir in the prawns.

Pour into a 1.2 litre (2 pint) capacity ring mould. Cover and chill in refrigerator until set, about 2 hours.

To serve, dip the base of the mould briefly in hot water and loosen with a knife. Turn onto a plate and fill the centre with watercress.

# Prawn custard vol-au-vents

**SERVES 6**

*12 medium vol-au-vent cases*
*175 g (6 oz) cooked peeled prawns,*
*    thawed if frozen*
*2 eggs*
*284 ml (10 fl oz) carton single*
*    cream*
*2 spring onions, finely chopped*
*1 tsp anchovy essence*
*2 tsp chopped fresh dill or fennel*
*salt and pepper*
*fennel sprigs, to garnish (optional)*

Heat the oven to 190°C, 375°F, Gas mark 5.

If the vol-au-vent cases are frozen, bake according to instructions, making sure that the shells remain intact. If already baked, arrange on a baking sheet, with 'lids' removed.

Pat the prawns dry, then divide between the vol-au-vent cases.

Whisk the eggs and cream in a bowl. Add the spring onions, anchovy essence, dill or fennel and seasoning. Spoon into the cases.

Bake for 15-20 minutes or until set. Replace 'lids' and serve hot. Garnish with fennel sprigs, if using.

● Salami and cheese cornets; Prawn custard vol-au-vents; Lobster and prawn mousse

# Hummus

**SERVES 6**

*432 g (15 oz) can chick peas,
    drained*
*1-2 garlic cloves, crushed*
*4 tbls sesame paste (tahini)*
*2 tbls olive oil*
*3 tbls lemon juice*
*½ tsp ground cumin*
*salt and pepper*
*2-3 tbls natural yoghurt or double
    cream*
*chopped parsley, to garnish
    (optional)*

Put the chick peas into a blender or food processor and add the garlic, sesame paste, oil, lemon juice, cumin and seasoning to taste. Blend until smooth. Add the yoghurt or cream and blend again briefly. Alternatively, mash chick peas with a potato masher or the back of a wooden spoon and beat in other ingredients.

Spoon the hummus into a serving dish and sprinkle with chopped parsley, if using.

**Serving idea:** Serve with warm pitta bread.

# Smokcd chccsc and apple appetizer

**SERVES 4**

*2 red-skinned apples, cored and
    cut into thin rings*
*175 g (6 oz) smoked cheese, any
    rind removed, thinly sliced*
*fresh mint sprigs and tomato slices,
    to garnish*
**For the dressing:**
*4 tbls vegetable oil*
*2 tbls cider vinegar*
*¼ tsp dry mustard*
*pinch of sugar*
*salt and pepper*

Shake the dressing ingredients in a screw-top jar until well mixed.

Toss the apple rings in a little of the dressing to prevent discoloration. Arrange the apple rings alternately with and slightly overlapping the cheese slices on a serving plate or individual plates. Pour over the remaining dressing and decorate with mint sprigs and tomato slices.

**Variations:** Use a mild crumbly goat's cheese instead of smoked cheese, and chopped fresh chives instead of mint. Add a little crushed garlic to the dressing, and garnish with fresh basil leaves.

# Crudités with spinach dip

**SERVES 6**

*300 g (11 oz) packet frozen
    chopped spinach, thawed*
*142 g (5 oz) full fat soft cheese with
    garlic and herbs, softened*
*1-2 tbls lemon juice or cider vinegar*
*3 tbls milk or natural yoghurt*
*selection of raw vegetables for
    dipping, such as carrot and
    celery sticks, cucumber chunks,
    cauliflower sprigs, endive leaves,
    radishes, cherry tomatoes*

Squeeze the spinach in your hands, a little at a time, to remove all excess water. Place the spinach in a blender or food processor and add the cheese, lemon juice or vinegar and milk or yoghurt. Blend until smooth. Taste and add more lemon juice if liked. Season if necessary. Spoon the dip into a bowl, cover and set aside at room temperature for 15 minutes for the flavours to blend.

Arrange the washed and sliced vegetables attractively on a platter and serve with the dip. Savoury biscuits may also be served.

● Hummus; Smoked cheese and apple appetizer; Crudités with spinach dip

# Devilled chicken livers

**SERVES 6**

450 g (1 lb) chicken livers, thawed
   if frozen
50 g (2 oz) butter
2 tbls Worcestershire sauce
6 tbls red wine or chicken stock
4 tsp Dijon mustard
Tabasco sauce
salt and pepper
unbuttered toast triangles, to serve
**To garnish:**
small tomato wedges
parsley sprigs

Prepare the chicken livers by removing any dark bits which will be bitter. Cut away any stringy pieces too. Chop the livers roughly.

Heat the butter in a large frying pan and cook the livers briskly until browned on all sides. Add the Worcestershire sauce, wine, mustard, a few drops of Tabasco sauce, and seasoning to taste. Stir to blend. Continue cooking until the livers are tender but still slightly pink in the centre.

Spoon the livers onto unbuttered toast triangles and garnish with small tomato wedges and parsley sprigs. Serve hot.

**Serving idea:** As a starter for a dinner party serve the cooked livers on a bed of salad leaves such as radicchio, curly endive and shredded round lettuce. The hot livers warm the salad leaves to create an unusual dish. Serve with warm bread and butter.

**Variation:** Cook the livers in 6 tbls of Madeira or dry sherry instead of wine or stock and replace the Tabasco sauce with lemon juice.

• Left: Devilled chicken livers; Above: Quick muffin pizzas

# Quick muffin pizzas

**SERVES 4**

*4 wholemeal muffins, split in half*
*198 g (7 oz) can tuna in oil, drained*
*and flaked, oil reserved*
*4 tsp tomato relish or pizza topping*
*sauce*
*215 g (7½ oz) can sliced*
*mushrooms, drained*
*50 g (2 oz) can anchovy fillets,*
*drained (optional)*
*225 g (8 oz) Mozzarella or Cheddar*
*cheese, grated*

Heat the grill to high.

Toast the flat side of the muffins until golden brown. Remove from the heat and turn them over. Brush lightly with oil from the can of tuna.

Spoon the tomato relish over the muffins, spreading it evenly to the edges. Top with the mushrooms, tuna and anchovies (if using). Divide the cheese between the muffins and press it on lightly.

Reduce the heat of the grill to moderately low and grill the 'pizzas' until they are heated through and the cheese on top has melted and is golden brown. Serve hot.

***Serving idea:*** Serve with a crisp, green salad of iceberg lettuce, sliced cucumber, diced green pepper and finely chopped spring onions.
***Variation:*** You can add a variety of toppings to these pizzas, the choice is endless. For instance, lightly mash a tin of sardines in tomato sauce and spread onto the base of the muffins, top with a mixture of diced tomatoes and chopped black olives. Sprinkle with grated cheese and cook as before.

The focal point of a menu is the second or main course, and in most cases the menu is planned around it. The accompaniments – hot vegetables or salad, a rice or pasta dish, or an interesting grain such as cous cous – are chosen to complement the ingredients in the main dish, and provide a nutritionally balanced meal.

What you select for the main dish, will depend on the occasion. For everyday and family meals, you'll want to choose something economical and nourishing, whereas for a special dinner party you may want to spend more time and to use more expensive ingredients. In both cases, you can take short-cuts to make meal preparation easier.

The recipes in this chapter show how you can take advantage of quick cooking methods, canned and packaged goods, ready-cooked meats, bottled sauces and other convenience foods as well as easily prepared raw fruits and vegetables to make main dishes suitable for any occasion.

In warm weather, salads, as main dishes make refreshing and healthy meals and are easy for the cook. From the delicatessen counter sliced turkey, ham and pork, whole roasted chicken, and salamis and other continental sausages can be combined with fresh fruits such as pineapple, grapes, melon, papaya, mango and avocado, as well as salad greens, canned beans, other vegetables, and imaginative dressings.

Quick hot casseroles can be made from delicatessen meats by mixing them with canned soups, pasta and rice, and frozen and canned vegetables. Canned fish and corned beef are also excellent short-cuts to use

in making hot main dishes.

In addition, fresh meats such as lamb and pork chops and minced beef can be cooked in or served with quickly made short-cut sauces.

Finishing touches can transform a short-cut dish into something really special, so thought should be given to the garnish. A sprig of parsley is often used to garnish a savoury dish but it is worth trying more adventurous garnishes – lemon, lime or orange slices or twists; nuts such as chopped peanuts or toasted flaked almonds; fresh herbs such as chives, lemon balm, mint, tarragon, basil or coriander, leafy salad vegetables such as watercress, and feathery tops of celery and fennel.

**These are a few more quick tips for main dishes:**

– Make a short-cut shepherd's pie with corned beef and onion as the base and instant mashed potatoes cheered up with herbs and grated cheese as the topping.
– Heat canned potatoes in a vinaigrette dressing and mix in thickly sliced German or French garlic sausage.
– Top grilled or fried steaks, chops or even fish fillets with a knob of pepper-flavoured soft cheese.
– Make up a white sauce using a packet mix and melt a large knob of herb and garlic flavoured cheese into the sauce. Pour onto chicken pieces and cook in the oven for 40 minutes until the chicken is cooked through.
– Marinate chicken pieces in bottled vinaigrette dressing, with extra herbs and garlic added, before baking, grilling or barbecuing.

# Salmon-stuffed croissants

**SERVES 4**

*198 g (7 oz) can pink salmon,
  drained and flaked*
*4 tbls mayonnaise*
*50 g (2 oz) Cheddar cheese, finely
  grated, reserving a little for
  garnish*
*4 pickled cocktail onions, finely
  chopped*
*8 stoned black or stuffed green
  olives, finely chopped*
*2 tbls chopped fresh parsley or
  1 tbls dried parsley*
*1-2 tsp lemon juice*
*4 croissants*

Heat the oven to 180°C, 350°F, Gas mark 4.

Mix together the salmon, mayonnaise, cheese, onions, olives, parsley and lemon juice until well blended.

Using a serrated bread knife, split open the croissants. Sandwich together with the salmon mixture. Arrange the stuffed croissants on a baking sheet. Sprinkle the reserved cheese on top. Bake for 7-10 minutes or until piping hot.

***Serving idea:*** Serve with a dry, white wine and a mixed salad.

● **Salmon-stuffed croissants**

# Mariner's lasagne

SERVES 4

12 sheets quick cook lasagne
198 g (7 oz) can tuna, drained and
  flaked
170 g (6 oz) can crabmeat, drained
175 g (6 oz) cooked peeled shrimps,
  thawed and drained if frozen
175-225 g (6-8 oz) Gruyère cheese,
  grated
For the sauce:
50 g (2 oz) butter or margarine
1 onion, finely chopped
1 small garlic clove, crushed
50 g (2 oz) flour
150 ml (¼ pint) dry white vermouth
  or dry white wine
450 ml (¾ pint) chicken stock,
  made from a stock cube
142 ml (5 fl oz) carton single cream
  or natural yoghurt
1 tsp dried mixed herbs
salt and pepper

Heat the oven to 190°C, 375°F, Gas
mark 5.

To make the sauce, heat the butter
in a saucepan; add the onion and
garlic. Cook until softened but not
brown. Stir in the flour, then add
the vermouth or wine and stock.
Bring to the boil, stirring, and simmer until thickened. Remove from
the heat and stir in the cream, herbs
and seasoning to taste.

Spoon a little sauce over the bottom of a 23 cm (9 inch) square
baking dish. Arrange a layer of four
lasagne sheets on top. Scatter over
half the tuna, crabmeat and
shrimps and one-third of the
cheese. Spoon over another layer of
sauce, then add another layer of
lasagne sheets. Add the remaining
seafood and another third of the
cheese. Cover with the remaining
lasagne sheets and spoon over the
rest of the sauce. Sprinkle the remaining cheese on top.

Bake for about 35 minutes or
until lightly browned on top and
bubbling. Serve hot.

*Variation:* Other seafood — fresh,
frozen or canned — may be used in
place of those suggested above. Even
smoked fish fillets can be used to
good effect. You can also use canned
salmon instead of tuna. As an
alternative make up a sauce using 2
packets of white wine sauce mix.
Combine with 600 ml (1 pint) liquid.

# Hot tuna-stuffed pears

SERVES 6

12 canned pear halves, preferably
  in unsweetened juice, drained
198 g (7 oz) can tuna in brine,
  drained
1 celery stalk, finely diced
2 spring onions, finely chopped
25 g (1 oz) stuffed green olives,
  sliced
75 g (3 oz) Cheddar cheese, finely
  grated
4 tbls mayonnaise
1 tbls cucumber relish
salt and pepper
watercress, to garnish

Heat the oven to 180°C, 350°F, Gas
mark 4.

Arrange the pears hollow side up,
in a shallow baking dish that is just
large enough to hold them comfortably side by side.

Combine the tuna, celery, spring
onions, olives, reserving a few for
decoration, cheese, mayonnaise,
cucumber relish, and seasoning to
taste in a mixing bowl. Use a fork to
blend the ingredients together thoroughly. Scoop the mixture into the
hollows in the pear halves, piling it
up and roughing it up with the fork.

Bake for 15-20 minutes or until
piping hot and the filling is lightly
browned at the edges. Serve hot,
garnished with sprigs of watercress
and slices of the reserved olives.

*Variation:* The tuna filling makes an
excellent sandwich spread. Serve it
cold, or make toasted sandwiches.

● Mariner's lasagne; Hot tuna-stuffed pears; Tuna Italian-style

# Tuna Italian-style

**SERVES 4**

1 large onion
2 × 198 g (7 oz) can tuna fish in oil
200 g (8 oz) mushrooms, sliced
25 g (1 oz) plain flour
397 g (14 oz) can chopped tomatoes
2 tsp dried basil
pinch of garlic salt
dash of Worcestershire sauce
pepper to taste
200 g (8 oz) spaghetti
4 tbls Parmesan cheese, finely
   grated

Fry the onion in a little of the oil drained from the tuna for 5 minutes or until soft. Add the mushrooms and fry for another 2 minutes.

Stir in the flour and cook for a further 2 minutes. Add the tomatoes and bring the sauce gradually to the boil, stirring continuously.

Add the basil, garlic salt, Worcestershire sauce, pepper and flaked tuna. Simmer for 5 minutes. Meanwhile, cook the pasta according to packet instructions.

Arrange pasta on serving plates, pour sauce over and sprinkle with Parmesan. Serve immediately.

23

# Chicken Florentine

**SERVES 4**

*40 g (1½ oz) butter, melted*
*300 g (11 oz) packet frozen*
  *chopped spinach, thawed and*
  *well drained*
*4 cooked chicken breasts, skinned*
  *and boned, or 350 g (12 oz)*
  *cooked chicken meat, shredded*
*295 g (10½ oz) can condensed*
  *cream of chicken soup*
*150 ml (5.29 oz) carton yoghurt*
*½ tsp mild curry paste*
*1 tsp lemon juice*
*pepper*
*50 g (2 oz) water biscuits, crushed*

Heat the oven to 180°C, 350°F, Gas mark 4.

Brush the bottom of a 1.2 litre (2 pint) capacity baking dish or casserole with 15 g (½ oz) of the butter. Spread the spinach over the bottom of the dish and arrange the chicken on top.

Mix together the undiluted soup, the yoghurt, curry paste, lemon juice and pepper to taste. Pour over the chicken. Mix the water biscuits with the remaining butter and sprinkle over the top.

Bake for about 30 minutes or until piping hot and lightly browned.

# Prawns Italienne

**SERVES 4**

*283 g (10 oz) can Napoletana sauce*
*450 g (1 lb) cooked, peeled prawns,*
  *thawed if frozen*
*2-3 tbls white wine*
*200 g (8 oz) tagliatelli or spaghetti*

Pour the sauce into a saucepan. Add the prawns and bring to the boil. Simmer for 5-10 minutes. Stir in the wine and cook for a further minute.

Meanwhile, cook the pasta according to packet instructions.

Arrange the pasta on serving dishes and spoon the sauce on top.

# Seafood gratin

**SERVES 4**

*450 g (1 lb) mixed seafood – see*
  *note below*
*450 ml (¾ pint) white wine sauce,*
  *made from a packet mix*
*2 tbls dry sherry*
*1 tbls creamed horseradish*
*dash of Worcestershire sauce*
*25 g (1 oz) Parmesan cheese,*
  *grated*
*25 g (1 oz) fresh breadcrumbs*
*15 g (½ oz) finely chopped mixed*
  *nuts – almonds, walnuts and*
  *peanuts or all almonds*

Heat the oven to 160°C, 325°F, Gas mark 3.

Remove any skin and bones from the fish and cut it into bite-size chunks. If using scallops, cut them into 2-3 pieces according to size. Cut lobster into bite-size pieces. Flake crabmeat.

Place the seafood in a mixing bowl and add the sauce, sherry, horseradish and Worcestershire sauce. Fold together gently but thoroughly.

Spoon the mixture into four individual gratin dishes or one large one and smooth the top. Mix together the cheese, breadcrumbs and nuts and sprinkle over the surface.

Bake for 30-35 minutes or until bubbling and golden brown.

*Note:* Choose fish steaks or cutlets such as cod, haddock, halibut, salmon, etc., or thick fillets. Or try a fish such as monkfish. Use 225-350 g (8-12 oz) of fish and make up to 450 g (1 lb) with cooked peeled prawns, fresh or frozen scallops (raw), cooked lobster or crabmeat or any canned seafood, including mussels.

● **Chicken Florentine; Seafood gratin; Prawns Italienne**

# Vegetable pilau

**SERVES 4**

*150 g (5 oz) brown rice*
*15 g (½ oz) butter*
*1 small onion, chopped*
*1 stick celery, chopped*
*50 g (2 oz) whole blanched*
*    almonds, chopped*
*375 g (13 oz) can ratatouille or*
*    equivalent amount of frozen*
*25 g (1 oz) grated cheese*

Cook the rice according to the packet instructions. When the rice is nearly cooked, melt the butter in a pan and sauté the onion and celery until soft. Add the almonds and ratatouille, stir and heat through.

Heat the grill to moderate. Arrange the cooked rice on a gratin dish and pile the vegetable mixture in the middle. Top with the grated cheese and cook under the grill until the cheese is melted.

# Rich spaghetti sauce

**SERVES 3-4**

*1 onion, finely chopped*
*1 green, yellow or red pepper,*
*    cored, seeded and diced*
*1 tbls vegetable oil*
*450 g (1 lb) lean minced beef*
*150 ml (¼ pint) red wine*
*425 g (15 oz) jar Napoletana-style*
*    spaghetti sauce*
**To serve:**
*hot freshly cooked spaghetti,*
*    tagliatelle or pasta shells*
*50 g (2 oz) grated cheese*

● **Vegetable pilau; Rich spaghetti sauce; Simple cheese fondue**

Cook the onion and diced pepper in the oil in a saucepan until soft and just beginning to brown. Add the beef and continue cooking until it is browned and crumbly, about 15-20 minutes. Stir and chop down frequently to break up the beef.

Add the wine and boil for about 10 minutes or until almost all evaporated.

Add the spaghetti sauce and stir to mix. Heat through and serve, spooned over hot pasta, with grated cheese to be sprinkled on top.

# Simple cheese fondue

**SERVES 6-8**

*225 g (8 oz) Gruyère cheese, grated*
*225 g (8 oz) Cheddar cheese,*
  *grated*
*1 clove garlic, skinned and halved*
*300 ml (½ pint) dry white wine*
*2 tsp cornflour*
*3-4 tsp milk*
*1 small liqueur glass Kirsch*
  *(optional)*
**To serve:**
*cooked ham, salami, etc., cut into*
  *fingers*
*cubes of French bread*
*gherkins*

Combine the cheeses in a bowl.

Rub the inside of a heavy saucepan with garlic, add the wine and bring to the boil. Gradually add the cheese mixture, stirring constantly. When all the cheese has been added and has melted, mix the cornflour to a smooth paste with a little milk and stir into the cheese mixture, add the liqueur, if using, and beat well. Cook, stirring for 1-2 minutes.

Pour into a cheese fondue pot and place over a burner. Each person dips meat and bread into the fondue using fondue forks or their fingers.

# Turkey and mushroom bake

**SERVES 4**

*100 g (4 oz) pasta shapes*
*350-450 g (12 oz-1 lb) cooked*
*turkey meat, cut into bite-size*
*pieces*
*213 g (7½ oz) can button*
*mushrooms, drained, or 225 g*
*(8 oz) fresh button mushrooms*
*295 g (10.4 oz) can condensed*
*cream of mushroom soup*
*1 celery stalk, diced*
*4 spring onions, chopped*
*150 g (5.29 oz) carton natural*
*yoghurt*
*pepper*
*50 g (2 oz) Cheddar cheese, grated*

Heat the oven to 180°C, 350°F, Gas mark 4.

Cook the pasta shapes in boiling, salted water until just tender. Drain well.

Combine the turkey, mushrooms, undiluted soup, celery, spring onions, yoghurt, pasta shapes and pepper to taste in a 1.75 litre (3 pint) baking dish or casserole. Stir well to mix.

Sprinkle the grated cheese over the turkey mixture. Bake for about 30 minutes or until piping hot and lightly browned on top.

**Serving idea:** Serve the Turkey and mushroom bake with a fresh green vegetable such as calabrese or broccoli.

# Barbecue beef baps

SERVES 4

25 g (1 oz) butter
1 onion, finely chopped
1 small green pepper, cored,
    seeded and sliced. Reserve a few
    slices for garnish and dice the
    remainder
1 garlic clove, crushed
3 tbls dark brown sugar
1 tbls Worcestershire sauce
1 tbls French mustard
6 tbls tomato ketchup
2 tbls cider vinegar
¼ tsp dried crushed chillies
salt and pepper
350 g (12 oz) cooked lean beef
4 baps or hamburger buns, split

Melt the butter in a saucepan and add the onion, green pepper and garlic. Cook until softened but not browned. Add the sugar, Worcestershire sauce, mustard, ketchup, vinegar, chillies. Season to taste and stir well. Cook over low heat for 10 minutes, stirring frequently.

Shred the beef and add to mixture. Stir well and heat through gently.

Spoon the beef mixture into the baps or buns and serve hot garnished with the reserved slices of pepper.

# Crispy chicken and sweetcorn savoury

SERVES 4

2 tbls cooking oil
2 small onions, chopped
2 × 418 g (14.7 oz) can chicken in
    white sauce
340 g (12 oz) can sweetcorn kernels
4 eggs, hard-boiled and chopped
50-75 g (2-3 oz) chopped walnuts
seasoning
3 small packets potato crisps,
    crushed

Heat the oil in a saucepan and fry the onion until soft. Add the chicken in white sauce, sweetcorn, eggs and walnuts. Heat gently and simmer for 5 minutes. Adjust the seasoning if necessary.

Transfer to a hot serving dish and top with crisps. Serve immediately with a side salad and bread rolls.

*Variation:* Add 2 sticks of celery cut into small slices with the sweetcorn, eggs and walnuts. Mix the crisp topping with some grated Gouda and pop under the grill until golden.

• Left: Turkey and mushroom bake
Centre: Barbecue beef baps
Right: Crispy chicken and sweetcorn savoury

# Curried ham and peach open sandwiches

SERVES 4

4 tbls mayonnaise
1 tsp mild curry paste
4 thin slices white or brown
  bread
4 slices smoked ham
4 canned peach halves
4 tsp mango chutney or sweet
  pickle

Heat the grill to moderate.

Mix together the mayonnaise and curry paste. Spread each slice of bread with about 2 tsp of the mayonnaise. Place a slice of ham on each slice of bread, cutting the ham to fit neatly. Top the ham with the peach halves, arranged hollow side up.

Fill the hollow in each peach half with 1 tsp chutney or pickle and top with a blob of the remaining curry mayonnaise.

Arrange the sandwiches on a baking sheet and place under the grill. Cook for about 4-5 minutes or until hot and bubbling. Serve hot and garnish the sandwiches with sprigs of parsley.

# Corned beef hash

SERVES 4

50 g (2 oz) butter
1 small onion, finely chopped
100 g (4 oz) corned beef, mashed
100 g (4 oz) cooked ham, diced
400 g (14 oz) can potatoes, drained
  and diced
100 g (4 oz) Cheddar cheese,
  grated
2 tbls chopped fresh parsley
1 tsp Worcestershire sauce
3 tbls tomato ketchup
½ tbls mild mustard
½ tbls creamed horseradish
4 eggs

Heat the oven to 160°C, 325°F, Gas mark 3.

Melt 25 g (1 oz) of the butter in a small frying pan and fry the onion until softened. Tip the onion into a mixing bowl. Add the corned beef, ham, potatoes, cheese, chopped parsley, Worcestershire sauce, ketchup, mustard and horseradish. Mix well together.

Spread the mixture in a shallow baking dish to about 2.5 cm (1 inch) deep. Smooth the top. Bake for 10-15 minutes.

Using the back of a large spoon, make four depressions in the corned beef mixture. Carefully break an egg into each hollow. Then melt the remaining butter and drizzle it over the eggs.

Return the dish to the oven and bake for a further 15-20 minutes or until the eggs are set and the corned beef hash is piping hot and bubbling, serve hot.

# Frankfurters with fruited rice

SERVES 4

25 g (1 oz) butter or margarine
1 medium onion, finely chopped
1 garlic clove, crushed
1 tbls flour
150 ml (¼ pint) chilli sauce or
  relish
1 tbls Worcestershire sauce
1 tsp French mustard
227 g (8 oz) can pineapple chunks,
  preferably in natural juice,
  drained and juice reserved
283 g (10 oz) can mandarin
  oranges, preferably in natural
  juice, drained and juice reserved
150 ml (¼ pint) orange juice
pepper
350-450 g (12 oz-1 lb) cooked
  brown or white rice – ordinary or
  quick-cook, or canned cooked rice
2 × 250 g (8.8 oz) traditional
  German sausage, skinned and
  thickly sliced

30

Heat the oven to 180°C, 350°F, Gas mark 4.

Melt the butter or margarine in a saucepan and fry the onion and garlic until softened. Sprinkle over the flour and stir in well, then add the chilli sauce or relish, Worcestershire sauce, mustard, juice drained from the pineapple chunks and mandarin oranges, orange juice and pepper to taste. Boil and simmer for 3 minutes, stirring frequently.

Put the rice and fruit into a bak-

● Top: Corned beef hash
Centre: Frankfurters with fruited rice
Bottom: Curried ham and peach open sandwiches

ing dish or casserole and add about half of the sauce. Fold together gently, then smooth the surface. Arrange the slices of sausage on top, and press into the rice mixture. Spoon over the remaining sauce.

Cover and bake for 30 minutes.

31

# Hawaiian kebabs

**SERVES 4**

*½ cucumber*
*2 bananas, peeled*
*8 pork sausages with herbs*
*1 medium red pepper (optional)*
*200 g (8 oz) streaky bacon*
*227 g (8 oz) can pineapple pieces,*
*    drained*

Preheat the grill to moderate.

Cut the cucumber into 2.5 cm (1 inch) slices then cut these in half.

Cut the bananas and sausages into 2.5 cm (1 inch) pieces and deseed and core the pepper, if using, into 2.5 m (1 inch) squares.

Derind the bacon and roll up each rasher.

Skewer all ingredients alternately onto 4 or 8 skewers (depending on their size).

Cook under the grill for about 15 minutes until the sausage and bacon are cooked, turning occasionally and basting with juice from the drained pineapple.

Serve on a bed of rice or noodles.

**Note:** Wrap the rashers of bacon around the banana pieces to prevent excessive browning.

# Island pork chops

**SERVES 4**

*4 large pork chops, trimmed*
*376 g (13.3 oz) can crushed*
*    pineapple*
*75 g (3 oz) light demerara sugar*
*200 ml (⅓ pint) fresh orange juice*
*4 tbls cider vinegar*
*1 tbls soy sauce*
*2 tbls ginger wine*
*25 g (1 oz) butter or margarine*
*mint or coriander leaves, to garnish*

Heat the oven to 180°C, 350°F, Gas mark 4.

Combine the pineapple (with juice), sugar, orange juice, vinegar, soy sauce, ginger wine and butter or margarine in a saucepan. Bring to the boil and simmer for about 20 minutes, stirring occasionally.

Arrange the chops in a baking dish that will hold them comfortably in one layer. Pour over the pineapple sauce. Bake for 45 minutes to 1 hour.

Serve garnished with mint or coriander leaves.

**Note:** If there is a lot of sauce in the dish at the end of the cooking time, thicken it with 1 tsp cornflour dissolved in 2 tsp water and cook for a further 2 minutes.

● **Left: Hawaiian kebabs**
**Top: Pizza frittata**
**Right: Island pork chops**

# Pizza frittata

**SERVES 4**

*6-8 eggs*
*5 tbls soured cream or natural*
*    yoghurt*
*salt and pepper*
*25 g (1 oz) butter or margarine*
*1 large Dutch tomato, thinly sliced*
*50 g (2 oz) salami or garlic*
*    sausage, cut into thin strips*
*50 g (2 oz) can anchovy fillets,*
*    drained*
*6-8 black olives*
*1 tsp mixed Italian seasoning herbs*
*100 g (4 oz) Mozzarella cheese,*
*    thinly sliced*

Heat the grill to moderate.

Lightly beat together the eggs, soured cream or yoghurt and seasoning to taste. Melt the butter or margarine in a 20 cm (8 inch) frying pan and pour in the egg mixture. Cook, lifting the set edges to let the liquid egg run onto the pan, until the omelette is set on the bottom but still somewhat runny on top. Remove from the heat.

Arrange the tomato slices, salami or garlic sausage, anchovies and olives on top of the omelette and sprinkle over the herbs. Top with the cheese slices.

Place the pan under the grill and cook until the cheese has melted and is beginning to brown. Serve hot, cut into wedges.

*Variation:* Almost any of your favourite pizza toppings can be used in this recipe: sliced mushrooms sautéed in butter, drained canned sardines, drained canned tuna, capers, other cheeses and so on.

● Texan cobbler; Savoury-filled garlic bread

# Texan cobbler

**SERVES 4**

1 tbls vegetable oil
1 small onion, finely chopped
225 g (8 oz) lean minced beef
2 × 400 g (14 oz) cans chilli beans
Tabasco sauce or dried crushed
   chillies (optional)
170 g (6 oz) packet scone mix
pinch cayenne pepper
4 tbls beer or water
50 g (2 oz) Edam cheese, finely
   grated
**To serve:**
shredded lettuce
sliced tomatoes
4 tbls soured cream or natural
   yoghurt

Heat the oven to 200°C, 400°F, Gas mark 6.

Heat the oil in a small frying pan and fry the onion until softened. Add the beef, and fry until browned and crumbly. Remove from the heat and drain off excess fat.

Add the beans, and Tabasco sauce or dried crushed chillies to taste, if liked. Stir to blend, then spoon into a 1.8 litre (3 pint) baking dish.

Mix together the scone mix, cayenne pepper, beer or water and half the cheese. Shape into 6 to 8 small rounds and place around the edge of the dish. Sprinkle with remaining cheese. Bake for 20-25 minutes until 'well risen' and golden.

Serve hot, with lettuce, tomatoes and soured cream or yoghurt.

# Savoury-filled garlic bread

**SERVES 4**

1 French baton loaf
50 g (2 oz) butter or margarine
  softened
1 tsp garlic salt
1 tsp dried chopped parsley
1 tsp lemon juice
**For the fillings:**
**Smoked sausage filling**
1 smoked sausage
2 tbls sweet pickle
**Hawaiian filling**
100 g (4 oz) full fat soft cheese
1 pineapple ring, chopped
50 g (2 oz) lean ham, chopped
**Crunchy peppery filling**
100 g (4 oz) full fat soft cheese
2 sticks celery, chopped
½ green pepper, finely chopped

Preheat oven to 200°C, 400°F, Gas mark 6.

Place the butter or margarine, garlic salt, parsley and lemon juice in a small bowl. Cream together with a fork.

Cut the bread in half lengthways and spread the butter mixture on each half.

Choose one of the fillings and use to sandwich the loaf together. To make any of the fillings simply mash all the ingredients together in a bowl until well incorporated. Wrap in foil and bake for 15 minutes. Remove from the oven, open the foil, then return to the oven for a further 5 minutes.

Cool slightly then cut into four portions. Serve hot or cold.

# Mango chicken

**SERVES 4-6**

*1.25 kg (2½ lb) whole cooked*
  *chicken*
*lettuce leaves*
*1 ripe mango*
*lime slice to garnish*
**For the dressing:**
*8 tbls natural yoghurt*
*2 tbls mango chutney*
*1 tsp lime juice*
*salt and pepper*

Remove the chicken meat from the carcass. Discard any gristle, skin and small bones, then cut the meat into bite-size cubes. Place them in a mixing bowl.

In another bowl, mix the dressing ingredients with seasoning. Add to the chicken cubes and toss to coat. Line a dish with lettuce leaves and top with the chicken.

Peel the mango. Cut the flesh away from the stone as neatly as possible, first cutting a few slices and reserving for decoration, then cut the remainder into cubes. Scatter mango around the chicken.

Garnish with a twist of lime and the reserved slices of mango.

# Chicken with melon

**SERVES 4-6**

*1.25 kg (2½ lb) whole cooked*
  *chicken*
*2 ripe sweet melons, such as Ogen,*
  *Charentais, etc.*
*2 celery stalks, diced*
*4 spring onions, finely chopped*
*lettuce leaves, shredded*
*1 ripe kiwi fruit, peeled and sliced*
  *crossways, to garnish*
**For the dressing:**
*3 tbls vegetable oil*
*1½ tbls cider or raspberry vinegar*
*½ tbls caster sugar*
*¼ tsp dry mustard*
*salt and pepper*

Remove the chicken meat from the carcass. Discard any gristle, skin and small bones, then cut the meat into bite-size cubes and place in a mixing bowl.

Cut the melons in half. Discard the seeds, then scoop out the flesh in balls using a special ball scoop, reserving the melon shells. Add the melon balls to the chicken with the celery and spring onions.

Shake all the dressing ingredients in a screw-top jar until well blended. Pour over the chicken salad and toss gently. Cover the bowl and chill for about 1 hour.

To serve, line the reserved melon shells with the shredded lettuce. Gently toss the salad and spoon into the melon shells. Garnish with the slices of kiwi fruit.

# Mexican-style chicken

**SERVES 6**

*1.25 kg (2½ lb) whole cooked
chicken*
*340 g (12 oz) can sweetcorn kernels
with peppers, drained*
*100 g (4 oz) mild cheese such as
Jarlsberg, Double Gloucester,
Doux de Montagne, etc., any rind
removed, dice*
*1 ripe avocado, peeled, stoned and
chopped*
*12 stuffed green olives, sliced*
*cos lettuce leaves*
*6 radishes, sliced*
**For the dressing:**
*6 tbls vegetable oil*
*3 tbls cider vinegar*
*1 garlic clove, crushed*
*1 tsp Mexican seasoning*
*salt and pepper*

Remove the chicken meat from the carcass. Discard any gristle, skin and small bones, then cut the meat into bite-size cubes. Place them in a mixing bowl.

Shake the dressing ingredients together, with seasoning to taste, in a screw-top jar. Pour the dressing over the chicken.

Add the sweetcorn, cheese, avocado, olives and radishes. Toss together gently. Cover and chill for about 1 hour.

Line a serving dish with lettuce leaves and pile the chicken mixture on top and garnish with radishes.

• **Left: Mexican-style chicken
Top: Mango chicken
Right: Chicken with melon**

# Turkey in tuna mayonnaise

**SERVES 4-6**

*50 g (2 oz) can rolled anchovy
   fillets with capers, drained*
*300 ml (½ pint) mayonnaise, or
   use half mayonnaise and half
   natural yoghurt*
*1 tbls capers*
*1 tbls lemon juice, or more to taste*
*99 g (3½ oz) can tuna, drained*
*pepper*
*12 large thinly sliced pieces of
   cooked turkey breast approx.
   350-450 g (12 oz-1 lb)*
**To garnish:**
*lemon slices*
*parsley sprigs*

Place six of the anchovy fillets, with their capers, in a blender or food processor. Add the mayonnaise, capers and lemon juice. Add the tuna. Blend until the sauce is smooth. Add pepper to taste and more lemon juice, if liked.

Spread about one-third of the sauce over the bottom of a serving dish. Roll up the turkey slices and arrange in the dish, in one layer if possible. Spoon over the remaining sauce so that the turkey can still be seen.

Garnish with lemon slices shaped into twists, parsley sprigs and the remaining rolled anchovy fillets. Cover the dish and chill in the refrigerator for about 1 hour before serving.

● Top: Spiced pork with papaya
Right: Smoked ham and bean salad
Below: Turkey in tuna mayonnaise

the oranges. Fold together gently. Cover and chill for about 1 hour.

Meanwhile, mix the mayonnaise and yoghurt with the orange rind. If the mixture is very thick, stir in the orange juice. Set aside to allow the flavours to mingle.

Thinly slice the remaining cucumber. Reserve one slice for the garnish, and arrange the rest over the bottom of a serving dish, overlapping the slices. Pile the ham and bean mixture on top and spoon over the orange mayonnaise. Garnish with the reserved slice of cucumber.

## Spiced pork with papaya

SERVES 4

*350 g (12 oz) cubed pork loin slices,*
*  rolled or shredded*
*1 large ripe papaya, peeled,*
*  seeded and cubed*
*Chinese leaves or lettuce, shredded*
*25 g (1 oz) flaked almonds, toasted*
**For the dressing:**
*6 tbls vegetable oil*
*3 tbls red wine vinegar*
*1 garlic clove, crushed*
*½ tsp ground cumin*
*¼ tsp dried crushed chillies*
*salt and pepper*

Combine the dressing ingredients in a mixing bowl and beat with a fork or whisk until well blended. Add the pork and papaya and toss to mix. Cover and leave to marinate at room temperature for about 1 hour.

To serve, make a bed of Chinese leaves or lettuce on a serving plate and spoon the pork and papaya mixture on top. Scatter over the toasted almonds.

## Smoked ham and bean salad

SERVES 4-6

*400 g (14 oz) can cannellini or*
*  butter beans, drained*
*225 g (8 oz) piece of smoked ham,*
*  cut into bite-size cubes*
*½ cucumber*
*298 g (11 oz) can mandarin*
*  oranges, drained*
*4 tbls mayonnaise*
*4 tbls natural yoghurt*
*½ tsp grated orange rind*
*1 tsp orange juice (optional)*

Place the beans and ham in a mixing bowl. Dice about one-quarter of the cucumber and add to the bowl with

# Chef's salad

**SERVES 4-6**

½ cos or iceberg lettuce
½ soft-leaved lettuce
1 head chicory, shredded
1 small bunch of watercress
½ cucumber, cut into small chunks
2 large Dutch tomatoes, or 4-6
    medium tomatoes, cut into
    wedges
225 g (8 oz) thickly-sliced mixed
    cooked meats such as ham,
    tongue, turkey, chicken,
    mortadella sauce, pastrami,
    cut into sticks or chunks
100 g (4 oz) Cheddar cheese, cut
    into sticks or chunks
100 g (4 oz) Gruyère cheese, cut
    into sticks or chunks
2 hard-boiled eggs, quartered
200 ml (⅓ pint) mayonnaise
4 tbls tomato-based chilli sauce or
    relish or hamburger relish

Tear the lettuces into bite-size pieces and place them in a large salad bowl with the chicory, watercress and cucumber. Toss together with your fingers.

Arrange the tomatoes, meats, cheeses, and eggs on top of the greens.

Lightly beat together the mayonnaise and chilli sauce or relish. Serve this dressing with the salad.

# Herbed beans with garlic sausage

**SERVES 4**

397 g (14 oz) can cannellini beans
397 g (14 oz) can red kidney beans
6 tbls olive oil
3 tbls cider vinegar
1 tsp Dijon mustard
2 tbls chopped fresh chives or
   spring onion tops
2 tbls chopped fresh parsley
1 tbls chopped fresh mint or ½ tbls
   dried mint
salt and pepper
1-2 tomatoes, sliced
mint sprigs, to garnish
225 g (8 oz) French garlic sausage
   or German salami-type sausage,
   sliced

● Left: Chef's salad
Above: Herbed beans with garlic
sausage

Tip the beans into a sieve and rinse under warm running water. Drain well.

Put the beans into a mixing bowl and add the oil, vinegar, mustard, chives or spring onion tops, parsley, mint and seasoning to taste. Toss with a spoon to blend.

Spoon into a serving dish and garnish with the tomato slices and mint sprigs. Serve with the sausage.

# PUGGINGS

Unless you are entertaining, it often seems a lot of trouble to make a pudding. There are times, of course, when you feel energetic enough to bake a cake or pie, and can take the time to enjoy making them, but it is more likely that you'll just opt for fruit, cheese and biscuits or a purchased dessert or ice cream at the end of a meal.

When a home-made dessert is required, but time is limited, you can use short-cuts to help you.

Ice cream can be turned into a sundae with a simply made sauce, or mixed with fruit jelly and set in a mould. Crushed digestive or ginger nuts make a quick base for a flan, and sponge fingers make layers of an instant 'gâteau'. Use maple syrup as an instant sauce for the popular pudding, crème caramel. Bought meringues and sponge or pastry flan cases can hold fillings made from canned and frozen fruits, melted marshmallows and instant dessert mixes. Cubes of frozen coffee can be whirled to a slush for a sophisticated Italian-style sorbet. Canned rice pudding topped with a quick butterscotch sauce and toasted flaked almonds makes another easy dessert.

Recipes using these ideas can be found in this chapter along with many others, but they can be adapted to suit your own taste and imagination.

**Here are a few more quick tips:**

— Add a splash of liqueur or spirit to ice cream or sorbet for a very special touch: try Grand Marnier or crème de menthe on vanilla ice cream, Tia Maria on chocolate ice cream, brandy on coffee ice cream, vodka on orange or lemon sorbet, and so on.
— Make a quick apple snow by folding 2 stiffly whisked egg whites, sugar to taste and a pinch of mixed spice into the contents of a jar or can of apple sauce.
— For a buttercream cake filling, blend a can of sweetened, chestnut purée or a jar of hazelnut chocolate spread with 175 g (6 oz) unsalted butter.
— Blend together 225 g (8 oz) ricotta or sieved curd cheese, 2-3 tbls icing sugar, 1 tbls brandy and a pinch of mixed spice and chill. Serve with sweet plain biscuits and fruits such as ripe peaches, apricots and plums.
— Gently melt a Mars bar and thin with milk or cream; pour over ice cream and sprinkle with chopped salted peanuts.
— Make a hot fruit compôte by combining 450 g (1 lb) dried prunes, 225 g (8 oz) dried apricots, a 439 g (15½ oz) can of pineapple (undrained), a 425 g (15 oz) can of cherries (undrained), 4 tbls medium or sweet white wine or sherry and 450 ml (¾ pint) water in a baking dish. Bake at 180°C/350°F/Gas 4 for 1½ hours, stirring occasionally.
— Dissolve a fruit jelly as directed, then stir in a can of fruit cocktail. Chill until thick then fold in whipped cream. Allow to set.
— Spread slices of bread with butter and place 4 tinned apricot halves on each piece. Sprinkle with icing sugar and place under a moderate grill until bread is toasted and crisp and apricots hot. Serve immediately.
— Soften orange sorbet and whisk in a little orange liqueur. Fold in canned mandarin orange segments, and freeze in a mould. Serve with brandy snap biscuits.

# Frozen cream moulds

**SERVES 4**

*2 tsp powdered gelatine*
*2 tbls water*
*175 g (6 oz) full fat soft cheese,*
  *softened*
*40 g (1½ oz) caster sugar*
*1 egg*
*1 tsp vanilla essence*
*142 ml (5 fl oz) carton soured cream*
**To serve:**
*fresh berries such as strawberries,*
  *raspberries, blackberries, etc.*
*strawberry leaves (optional)*

● **Frozen cream moulds**

Sprinkle the gelatine over the water in a small heatproof bowl. Leave for 2-3 minutes until spongy. Stand bowl in a pan of hot water until dissolved. Remove from heat and cool slightly.

Cream the cheese with the sugar until smooth. Beat in the egg and vanilla essence. Stir in the gelatine, then fold in the soured cream.

Divide the mixture between four small moulds or individual ramekins. Cover and freeze until set (about 3-4 hours).

Just before serving, dip the bottoms of the moulds or ramekins in hot water and turn out the creams onto serving plates. Add berries, and a few strawberry leaves, if wished.

# Red wine cream

SERVES 4-6

*1 packet raspberry jelly*
*300 ml (½ pint) boiling water*
*150 ml (¼ pint) red wine*
*284 ml (10 fl oz) carton double*
  *cream*
*fresh raspberries, to decorate*

Dissolve the jelly in the boiling water and add the red wine. Leave in the refrigerator to cool but not set.

Beat the cream until it forms stiff peaks and gradually fold in the jelly.

Pour into individual serving dishes and leave for 4-5 hours or overnight in the refrigerator to set.

Before serving, decorate with fresh raspberries.

# Maple cream

SERVES 6-8

*175 g (6 oz) full fat soft cheese,*
  *softened*
*50 g (2 oz) caster sugar*
*½ tsp vanilla essence*
*4 large eggs*
*300 ml (½ pint) milk*
*6-8 tbls pure maple syrup*
*slice of orange, to garnish*

Heat the oven to 180°C, 350°F, Gas mark 4.

Place the soft cheese, sugar and vanilla essence in a food processor and blend briefly until smooth. Add the eggs and blend again, then blend in the milk. If the mixture is frothy, stir until bubbles subside.

Alternatively, cream the cheese with a wooden spoon until it is soft, then beat in the sugar and vanilla essence. Beat in the eggs, one at a time. Mix in the milk.

Pour the maple syrup into a 20 cm (8 inch) round baking dish and tilt the dish so that the syrup covers the bottom evenly. Slowly pour the cheese custard into the dish.

Place the dish in a roasting tin and add enough hot water to the tin to come halfway up the sides of the dish. Bake for about 35 minutes or until the custard is just set.

Remove dish from oven and allow to cool, then chill well to set.

To serve, run a knife around the edge of the cream to loosen it from the dish. Turn out onto a shallow, lipped serving dish, large enough to allow space for the syrup to pool around the cream. As a decoration, place an orange slice on top.

# Bananas Melba

SERVES 4

*175 g (6 oz) seedless raspberry jelly*
*142 ml (5 fl oz) carton single cream*
*¼ tsp mixed spice*
*50 g (2 oz) frozen or canned*
  *raspberries*
*4 ripe bananas*
*8 scoops vanilla ice cream*
*4 tbls crushed coconut macaroons*

Melt the jelly in a saucepan over a moderate heat, stirring frequently. Remove from the heat and whisk in the cream and spice. Allow to cool. If the sauce has any small lumps of unmelted jelly in it, sieve these out. Mash the raspberries with a fork and fold into the sauce. Chill the sauce until ready to serve.

Peel the bananas and halve them lengthways. Arrange two halves side by side on each of four banana split or other long individual serving dishes. (Alternatively, the bananas may be sliced crossways and put in bowls.) Put two scoops of ice cream on each serving. Spoon over the sauce and sprinkle with the crushed biscuits. Serve immediately.

• **Maple cream; Bananas melba; Red wine cream**

# Butterscotch rice dessert

**SERVES 4**

2 × 439 g (15.5 oz) cans creamed
  rice pudding
2 large ripe nectarines, stoned and
  sliced, or 410 g (14½ oz) canned
  sliced peaches, drained
toasted flaked almonds
**For the sauce:**
50 g (2 oz) golden syrup
75 g (3 oz) light brown sugar
25 g (1 oz) butter
pinch of salt

First make the sauce. Combine the syrup, sugar, butter and salt in a heavy saucepan and bring to the boil, stirring to dissolve the sugar and melt the butter. Set aside to cool slightly while you warm the rice pudding.

Tip the cans of pudding into another saucepan and heat through gently, stirring occasionally.

Spoon the pudding into four individual serving bowls. Top with the nectarine or peach slices and spoon over the sauce. Sprinkle toasted flaked almonds on top and serve.

*Note:* This sauce, with the almonds, is excellent with vanilla ice cream.

# Strawberry cheese flan

**SERVES 4-6**

½ packet strawberry jelly
150 ml (¼ pint) boiling water
1 tbls caster sugar
100 g (4 oz) full fat soft cheese, at
  room temperature
142 ml (5 fl oz) carton soured cream
  or natural yoghurt
18-20 cm (7-8 inch) sponge flan
  case
12 medium strawberries, sliced
2 tbls redcurrant jelly
small strawberry leaf, to garnish

Put the strawberry jelly in a mixing bowl and pour over the boiling water. Stir until the jelly has melted. Add the sugar and stir until dissolved. Allow to cool.

Add the cheese and soured cream or yoghurt and whisk until blended and smooth. Chill in the refrigerator until thick.

Remove from the refrigerator and whisk the mixture, then spoon into the flan case and smooth the top. Arrange the strawberry slices over the surface, slightly overlapping them. Warm the redcurrant jelly until it has melted, then brush or spoon it over the strawberry slices to glaze them. Chill for about 1 hour and then decorate with a small strawberry leaf before serving with pouring cream or yoghurt.

# Instant baked Alaska

**SERVES 4**

● Butterscotch rice dessert; Strawberry cheese flan; Instant baked Alaska

*18-20 cm (7-8 inch) sponge
  flan case
4 tbls sweet sherry or brandy
2 egg whites
¾ tsp vanilla essence
¼ tsp cream of tartar
50 g (2 oz) caster sugar
1 family sized tub vanilla ice
  cream*

Heat the oven to 200°C, 400°F, Gas mark 6.

Arrange the flan case on a baking sheet and sprinkle with the sherry or brandy. Set aside.

Combine the egg whites, vanilla essence and cream of tartar in a mixing bowl. Beat with a whisk until it forms soft peaks, then gradually beat in the caster sugar. Continue beating until the meringue is very thick and glossy and will hold a peak when the beaters are lifted out.

Empty the tub of ice cream onto the flan case and if necessary shape the ice cream to form a mound and cover the base of the flan. Cover with the meringue, swirling it all over to cover the ice cream and flan completely.

Place in the oven and cook until the meringue is lightly tinged beige all over, about 2-3 minutes. Serve immediately.

*Variation:* Use 4 individual flan cases if large ones are unavailable.

47

# Iced apricot mousse pie

**SERVES 6-8**

¹/₂ × 200 g (7 oz) packet gingernut
    biscuits, crushed
75 g (3 oz) apricot jam, warmed
425 g (15 oz) can apricots,
    preferably in natural juice,
    drained
2 egg whites
100 g (4 oz) caster sugar
5 tbls whipped cream or thick
    natural yoghurt
1 tsp lemon juice
**To garnish:**
whipped cream
crystallised ginger (optional)

Mix together the crushed biscuits and jam until well combined. Press over the bottom of a 20 cm (8 inch) springform tin that has been lined with a round of greaseproof paper. It is easiest to use a dampened spoon or fingers to press out the mixture as it is sticky. Set aside.

Purée the apricots in a blender, food processor or sieve. In a bowl, whisk the egg whites until stiff. Gradually add the sugar whisking continuously until the mixture is thick and glossy.

Add the whipped cream or yoghurt stirring gently until well incorporated. Fold in the apricot purée and lemon juice.

Pour the apricot mixture over the biscuit base and spread it out smoothly. Cover and freeze until firm, about 4 hours.

About 10 minutes before serving, transfer the pie to the refrigerator so

that it can soften slightly. Unclip the side of the tin and slide the pie from the base onto a serving plate. Decorate the top of the pie with crystallised ginger or whipped cream, if liked.

# Pineapple cream pie

SERVES 6

*142 ml (5 fl oz) carton soured cream*
*or natural yoghurt*
*376 g (13.3 oz) can crushed*
*pineapple, drained*
*1 packet peach flavoured instant*
*pudding mix*
*20 cm (8 inch) baked pastry case,*
*bought or homemade*
*whipped cream, to decorate*
*(optional)*

Combine the soured cream or yoghurt and juice of drained pineapple in a mixing bowl. Add the pudding mix and beat lightly with a whisk until well blended. Fold the crushed pineapple into the mixture.

Spoon the pineapple mixture into the pastry case and spread evenly.

If liked, decorate with swirls of whipped cream.

# Creamy ginger cheesecakes

SERVES 4

*2 tsp powdered gelatine*
*2 tbls water*
*8 slices Jamaican ginger cake*
*2 tbls ginger marmalade*
**For the topping:**
*150 g (6 oz) full fat soft cheese*
*142 ml (5 fl oz) carton single cream*
*1 tbls ginger marmalade*
*1 tsp ground ginger*
*1 egg, separated*
*chopped stem ginger or grated*
*chocolate, to decorate*

Sprinkle the gelatine over the water in a small heatproof bowl. Leave for 2-3 minutes until spongy. Stand bowl in a pan of hot water until the gelatine has dissolved. Remove from heat and cool slightly.

Spread each slice of cake with marmalade and use to line 4 individual glass dishes. Trim to fit and press down well.

To make the topping, mix together the cheese, cream, marmalade and ground ginger then beat in the egg yolk. Whisk egg white until stiff and fold into the cheese mixture. Stir in the gelatine.

Pour the topping over the cake slices. Chill until set.

Decorate with chopped stem ginger or grated chocolate.

---

● Pineapple cream pie; Creamy ginger cheesecakes; Iced apricot mousse pie

## Peach and almond crumble

SERVES 4

410 g (14½ oz) can of peach slices
  in natural juice, drained
50 g (2 oz) flaked almonds, toasted
227 g (8 oz) packet crumble
  topping
25 g (1 oz) ground almonds

Heat the oven to 200°C, 400°F, Gas mark 6.

Put the peaches and half the drained juice into an oval dish. Sprinkle the toasted almond flakes on top.

Mix the crumble topping with the ground almonds and cover the peaches. Place in the centre of the oven and cook for 20-25 minutes until golden brown.

**Serving idea:** Reserve a few of the toasted almonds and when crumble is cooked, sprinkle on top.

## Strawberry fluff

SERVES 4

4 egg whites
4 tbls icing sugar
4 × 142 ml (5 fl oz) strawberry
  yoghurt
4 tsp crunchnut topping, to decorate

Whisk the egg whites until stiff. Add the icing sugar and whisk again until the mixture forms stiff peaks. Fold in the yoghurt.

Spoon into individual dishes and decorate with crunchnut topping. Serve immediately.

# Quick coffee crush

**SERVES 4**

*600 ml (1 pint) boiling water*
*4 tbls instant coffee powder or*
*    granules*
*4 tbls caster sugar*
*4 tbls Tia Maria or Kahlua*
*whipped cream, to decorate*

Stir together the water, coffee and sugar until the coffee and sugar have dissolved. Allow to cool, then pour into two ice cube trays with dividers. Freeze until solid, about 3 hours.

About 5 minutes before serving, remove the ice cube trays from the freezer and allow the coffee ice cubes to soften slightly.

Tip the cubes into a food processor and whirl to a slush. If you do not have a food processor, allow the cubes to soften for 10 minutes, then beat to a slush with electric beaters.

Spoon the coffee slush into glasses, and pour over the coffee liqueur. Top each serving with a whirl of whipped cream. Serve immediately.

*Note:* Strong percolated or filtered coffee may be used instead of instant coffee and water.

---

• Peach and almond crumble; Quick coffee crush; Strawberry fluff

---

# Rich chocolate almond gâteau

**SERVES 6-8**

175 (6 oz) unsalted butter
75 g (3 oz) muscovado or soft
   brown sugar
175 g (6 oz) plain chocolate
100 g (4 oz) ground almonds
2 tbls brandy
284 ml (10 fl oz) carton double
   cream
2 tbls water
24-28 sponge fingers

Cream together the butter and sugar. Melt the chocolate in a bowl over a pan of hot water. Mix the chocolate, almonds and 1 tbls brandy into the butter mixture.

Whip the cream until thick and fold half of it into the chocolate almond mixture.

Line the bottom and sides of a 1 kg (2 lb) loaf tin with greaseproof paper.

Mix the remaining brandy with the water in a shallow dish. Dip the unsugared side of each biscuit into the liquid – just to moisten, not to saturate – and arrange the biscuits, sugared side down and side by side, in a layer on the bottom of the tin. There should be room for a layer of 8 biscuits.

Spoon over half the chocolate mixture and spread it out evenly. Make another layer of moistened biscuits, then spread over the remaining chocolate mixture. Cover with a layer of the remaining biscuits.

Cover the tin and chill in the refrigerator until the gâteau is firm, about 1 hour. For speed, the chilling may be done in the freezer.

When ready to serve, turn the gâteau out of the tin on to a serving plate and peel off the lining paper. Smooth the sides with a knife dipped in hot water. Serve with the remaining whipped cream. Alternatively, use the cream to decorate the chocolate almond gâteau.

# Minted cream meringues

**SERVES 6**

65 g (2½ oz) large white
   marshmallows – about 16
6 tbls milk
2-3 tbls Crème de Menthe
142 ml (5 fl oz) carton double
   cream
6 individual bought meringue nests
**To decorate:**
4 small sprigs fresh mint
little lightly beaten egg white
little caster sugar

Place the marshmallows and milk in a heavy saucepan and melt over a low heat, stirring frequently. When smooth, remove from the heat and allow to cool. Stir in the Crème de Menthe.

Whip the cream until thick and whisk gently into the marshmallow mixture. Cover and chill until very thick, about 2-3 hours.

Meanwhile, make the decoration. Wipe the mint sprigs and pat dry. Using a small paint brush, brush the mint leaves with beaten egg white (beaten just until frothy), or just dip the leaves in the egg white and shake off the excess. Then dip the leaves in the caster sugar to coat lightly. Set the sprigs aside to dry for about 15 minutes.

When ready to serve, pipe or spoon – using an ice cream scoop if liked – the marshmallow mixture into the meringue nests. Decorate each with a frosted mint sprig.

*Variation:* Other liqueurs may be used to flavour the cream, e.g. coffee, orange, chocolate. Decorate with the corresponding fruit or grated chocolate.

---

● **Top: Rich chocolate almond gâteau
Centre: Minted cream meringues
Below: Apricot-topped almond
shortbread**

---

# Apricot-topped almond shortbread

**SERVES 6**

*6 shortbread biscuits*
*2 drops almond essence or almond*
  *liqueur*
*425 g (15 oz) can apricot halves*
*142 ml (5 fl oz) carton clotted or*
  *extra thick cream*
*1 tbls flaked almonds*

Place the shortbread biscuits on 6 individual plates. Mix the almond essence or liqueur with about 2 tbls of the apricot juice and pour 1 tsp over each piece of shortbread to moisten slightly.

Spread thickly with cream.

Cut apricot halves into thin slices and arrange decoratively on top of the cream.

Arrange or sprinkle with flaked almonds and serve immediately.

If your life is hectic, with busy days at work and evenings devoted to favourite sports or leisure activities, having friends over to lunch or dinner may seem a bit of a chore. But with some careful planning and organization, and the judicious use of short-cuts in the kitchen, entertaining can be a real pleasure.

Start by planning your menu. Take note of seasonal fruits and vegetables, and special offers on meat, poultry or fish. Check on your friends' preferences, too, if possible. They may be on a diet, or cutting out meat, or allergic to shell-fish.

Choose dishes that will enable you to spend as much time as possible out of the kitchen and with your guests. This means doing as much as you can ahead of time, and avoiding having several dishes that need your attention at the last minute.

An ideal combination is a cold starter that can be prepared ahead of time and a hot main dish that will carry on cooking happily while you prepare its accompaniments. A hot soup that only needs reheating is a good first course, too, as is any hot appetizer that can be prepared in advance and cooked just before serving.

The same guidelines apply to desserts – whether prepared well ahead to be served cold, or, if requiring last-minute attention, following a simple main dish.

Once your menu is planned, make a detailed shopping list. Also plan what you can prepare the day before or several hours in advance. It's helpful, too, to work out a timetable for the final preparation and cooking therefore dispensing with those last minute panics.

Do any cleaning and set the table so that these tasks are out of the way before you put on your apron. Flowers on the table are a nice touch, so add flowers to your shopping list if there's nothing in your garden.

It's a good idea to make extra ice cubes for drinks. Tip frozen cubes into a freezer bag and tie closed; return it to the freezer with the freshly filled ice cube trays. A special touch for drinks is to freeze leaves of fresh herbs such as mint and lemon balm or small flowers or rose petals in the ice cubes. For cool summer drinks, freezing pieces of fruit into ice-cubes makes for a refreshing change. For instance, raspberries, cherries, half a strawberry, a cube of kiwi; a slice or cube of peach.

A punch served before the meal is an easier – and more economical – alternative to offering a selection of drinks. Remember that salty finger foods such as nuts and crisps will make your guests thirstier.

Try this quick curried nut recipe: combine 4 tbls olive oil, 1 tbls curry powder, 1 tbls Worcestershire sauce and a pinch of cayenne pepper in a frying pan. Heat and add 225 g (8 oz) blanched almonds, walnut halves, shelled unroasted peanuts or pecan nut halves (or a mixture of nuts) and stir until the nuts are well coated with the spice mixture. Tip onto a baking sheet and spread out, then bake at 150°C/300°F/Gas 2 for 10 minutes. Cool before serving.

Another interesting and quick hors d'oeuvre to serve with drinks is your own marinated olives. Drain a can or jar of black olives and place in a clean screwtop jar. Add 1-2 peeled garlic cloves, the thinly pared rind of an orange and sprigs of fresh herbs such as rosemary and thyme. Add enough olive oil (or a mixture of olive and sunflower or safflower oil) to the jar to come level with the olives. Cover the jar and leave the olives to marinate for at least a day. Shake the jar occasionally, and drain the olives for serving.

Cheese straws can be made very quickly using purchased fresh or frozen puff pastry. Roll out the pastry thinly and sprinkle with grated Parmesan cheese. Fold the pastry in half and roll out again. If you like, sprinkle with Parmesan once more, fold in half and roll out again. Cut into strips, arrange on a baking sheet and bake at 200°C/400°F/Gas 6 for about 10 minutes, or until crisp and golden brown. Cool before serving.

Make a quick dip by mashing an avocado with 1 tbls of lemon juice. Cream together 100 g (4 oz) low fat soft cheese with a dash of Worcestershire sauce, salt and cayenne pepper and ½ tbls of grated onion. Beat into the avocado mixture. Serve with sticks of cucumber, carrots, celery and florets of cauliflower.

Some kinds of entertaining are more relaxing than others. A barbecue, for example, means just as much preparation for the cook, but guests often like to help with the cooking. You can even plan a 'cook-your-own' barbecue, with the raw ingredients for kebabs or hamburgers set out and guests encouraged to select and cook their own meal. A delicious and very quick sauce to serve with barbecued kebabs is to combine ½ cucumber, diced, 1 clove of garlic, crushed, 1 tsp cider vinegar and crushed, fresh mint leaves with 2 × 150 g (5.29 oz) cartons natural yoghurt. Leave in the refrigerator to chill and for the flavours to combine. A fondue party also involves everyone in cooking, and is lots of fun for all concerned.

A wine and cheese party is the simplest kind of buffet. A good selection of cheeses, some meats from the delicatessen counter, gherkins, olives, unsalted butter and crusty bread can all be purchased. You can buy a ready-made quiche and spice it up by adding slices of tomato and a sprinkling of herbs and popping it into the oven. Serve wedges of quiche warm.

More elaborate buffets can have their short-cuts, too, with the use of convenience foods and delicatessen goods. Some suitable first course recipes for a buffet are: Salami and cheese cornets (page 14), Egg and caviar mould (page 12), Rollmops with apple and beetroot (page 13), Smoked fish pâté (page 11), Curried tuna pâté (page 13), Hummus (page 16) and Lobster and prawn mousse (page 14).

Second courses suitable for a cold buffet are: Turkey in tuna mayonnaise (page 38), Chef's salad (page 40), Chicken with melon (page 36), Spiced pork with papaya (page 39), and Mango chicken (page 36).

Buffet desserts could include: Minted cream meringues (page 52), Strawberry cheese flan (page 46), Raspberry orange delights (page 63), Rich chocolate almond gâteau (page 52) and Chocolate liqueur pots (page 57).

If you are serving coffee and tea at the end of the meal, it can save time to have the cups and saucers, teaspoons, sugar and jug for cream or milk on a tray, ready to be taken to the table when required. With coffee it is a delicious treat to serve sweets such as crisp after dinner chocolate sticks or peppermint creams.

Finally, in all your planning, allow a little time for yourself. This is one place not to take a short-cut. Most importantly, when all advance preparations are completed in the kitchen, the table is set and your home ready to receive your guests, don't forget to set a small amount of time aside and allow yourself to relax and change. You'll then be confident that all is ready and waiting, and can enjoy the occasion fully.

## CELEBRATION DINNER

*Spinach, avocado and pâté salad*

*Lamb chops with orange cream sauce*

*Chocolate liqueur pots*

•

*Sauvignon*

*Vin de Pays Côtes Catalan*

# Lamb chops with orange cream sauce

SERVES 4

8 lamb chops
3 tbls orange juice
6 tbls dry white wine
2 tbls orange marmalade
4 tbls single cream
salt and pepper
1 tbls orange liqueur (optional)
2 tbls chopped fresh chives
1 orange, sliced

Heat the grill.

Arrange the chops on the grill rack and brush them with a little of the orange juice. Grill the chops until golden brown on both sides, and cooked to your liking (turning as

# Spinach, avocado and pâté salad

SERVES 4

225 g (8 oz) fresh young spinach
    leaves or soft-leaved lettuce
100 g (4 oz) liver pâté
2 ripe avocados, peeled, stoned
    and sliced
4 medium tomatoes, quartered, or
    20 cherry tomatoes (Gardener's
    Delight)
**For the dressing:**
3 tbls olive oil
1 tbls dry white wine or vermouth
½ tbls lemon juice
½ garlic clove, crushed
1 tsp whole grain mustard such as
    Moutarde de Meaux

Rinse the spinach or lettuce leaves and pat dry with kitchen paper towels. Cut the pâté into 8 slices.

Shake together the ingredients for the dressing in a screw-top jar.

Toss the avocado slices in a little of the dressing to prevent discoloration.

Arrange the spinach or lettuce, pâté, avocado and tomatoes decoratively on individual plates. Sprinkle over the remaining dressing and serve, with warmed French bread.

necessary), and brushing with the orange juice from time to time.

Meanwhile, combine the wine and marmalade in a small saucepan. Bring to the boil, stirring to melt the marmalade. Add the cream and seasoning to taste. Boil until the liquid has reduced by half and is saucelike. Remove from the heat and stir in the liqueur, if liked.

Pour the sauce on to a serving platter and place the chops on top. Sprinkle with the chives. Garnish with the orange slices and serve.

# Chocolate liqueur pots

**SERVES 4**

175 g (6 oz) plain chocolate
2 large eggs
1 tbls brandy or liqueur
142 ml (5 fl oz) carton single cream
**To decorate:**
whipped cream
cocoa powder

Break up the chocolate into small pieces and place in a food processor. Add the eggs and brandy or liqueur. Blend briefly.

Warm the cream in a small saucepan until bubbles begin to appear around the edge. Pour the cream into the processor and blend until the mixture is smooth and evenly coloured.

Divide the chocolate mixture between four ramekins or other small individual serving dishes. Cover and chill until firm, about 2 hours.

When ready to serve, decorate each pot with whipped cream and a sprinkle of cocoa powder.

● Left: Spinach, avocado and pâté salad
Right: Lamb chops with orange cream sauce
Top: Chocolate liqueur pots

Place salmon in blender or food processor with the mayonnaise, yoghurt and pepper to taste. Blend until well mixed. Or dice the salmon finely and beat into the mayonnaise and yoghurt. Add pepper to taste.

Put one mackerel fillet on each of four individual serving plates, or all on a large serving plate. Place a spoonful of smoked salmon mayonnaise alongside each mackerel.

Garnish with cucumber slices, watercress and lemon wedges.

*Variation:* Serve the smoked salmon mayonnaise with hard-boiled eggs.

● Smoked mackerel with smoked salmon mayonnaise; Peanut and pineapple chicken

# Smoked mackerel with smoked salmon mayonnaise

**SERVES 4**

*25 g (1 oz) smoked salmon*
*4 tbls mayonnaise*
*4 tbls natural yoghurt*
*pepper*
*4 smoked mackerel fillets*
**To garnish:**
*cucumber slices*
*watercress*
*lemon wedges*

# Peanut and pineapple chicken

### SERVES 4

2 small ripe pineapples
450 g (1 lb) cooked chicken meat,
    cut into bite-size cubes
2 celery stalks, diced
225 g (8 oz) seedless green grapes
**For the dressing:**
5 tbls peanut butter, crunchy or
    smooth
5 tbls mayonnaise
5 tbls natural yoghurt
1 garlic clove, crushed
1 tsp curry powder
1 tbls apricot jam
**To garnish:**
chopped fresh chives
coarsely chopped salted peanuts

Using sharp scissors, trim any brown tips from the green crown of leaves on the pineapples. Cut each pineapple in half lengthways, through the crown of leaves. Remove the flesh from each half; discard the core. Cut into bite-size pieces.

Combine the pineapple flesh, chicken, celery and grapes in a mixing bowl. Set the four pineapple skin 'boats' aside.

Put all the ingredients for the dressing in a mixing bowl and beat with a wooden spoon or electric mixer until thoroughly blended.

Add the dressing to the chicken and pineapple mixture and fold together. The dressing will be thick, but will become more liquid as it blends with the pineapple juices.

Spoon the chicken salad into the pineapple 'boats', piling it up. Mix together the chives and peanuts and sprinkle over the top.

# Berry sponge creams

**SERVES 4**

1 packet fruit-flavoured instant
  pudding mix (flavour should
  match your fresh berries)
300 ml (½ pint) milk
100 g (4 oz) sponge fingers coarsely
  crushed
225 g (8 oz) fresh berries in season
  or frozen berries, thawed and
  well drained, or 425 g (15 oz) can
  fruit, reserving a few for
  decoration
4 tbls Crème de Cassis or Grand
  Marnier (optional)

Make up the pudding with the milk,
according to the instructions on the
packet.

Divide the crushed biscuits between four dessert glasses, reserving
about 4 tsp of the biscuits for the
topping. Pile the berries on top of
the biscuits and sprinkle with the
liqueur, if using. Spoon the pudding
on top and sprinkle with the reserved biscuits and berries.

**Variation:** As an alternative to
sponge fingers use gingernuts,
macaroons or ratafias.

● Berry sponge creams

# Japanese seafood salad

**SERVES 4**

*1 cucumber*
*salt*
*150 ml (¼ pint) rice vinegar*
*1 tbls caster sugar*
*170 g (6 oz) can crabmeat, drained*
*175 g (6 oz) cooked peeled prawns, thawed and drained if frozen*

Peel the cucumber and reserve some of the skin. Cut the reserved skin into very thin strips and set aside for the garnish.

Sprinkle a work surface liberally with salt and roll the cucumber in it, pressing the salt in on all sides. This will soften the cucumber very quickly. Rinse off the salt and pat the cucumber dry with kitchen paper towels. Cut the cucumber into thin slices.

Combine the vinegar and sugar in a mixing bowl and stir until the sugar has dissolved. Add the crabmeat and prawns and fold together gently.

Arrange the cucumber slices decoratively on individual plates. Using a fork, pile the seafood mixture in the centre. Spoon the vinegar dressing over the cucumber. Garnish with the strips of cucumber skin, and chill for about 30 minutes before serving.

*Variation:* If Japanese rice vinegar is unavailable, use 6 tbls cider vinegar, 4 tbls water and 2 tbls caster sugar.

• Japanese seafood salad

# Stir-fried pork with vegetables

**SERVES 4**

350 g (12 oz) pork fillet, cut into
    thin strips
2 tbls vegetable oil
1 garlic clove, crushed
2 tsp finely chopped fresh root
    ginger
1 celery stalk, thinly sliced
1 red pepper, thinly sliced
3 spring onions, thinly sliced
225 g (8 oz) mushrooms, thinly
    sliced
230 g (8 oz) can water chestnuts,
    drained and thinly sliced
2 tbls soy sauce
2 tbls sherry
1 tsp stem ginger, chopped with its
    sauce
pinch of cayenne pepper
1 tsp cornflour

Heat the oil in a large frying pan or wok. Add the pork and stir-fry over high heat until it is pale in colour and beginning to brown. Remove the pork with a slotted spoon.

Add the garlic, ginger, celery, red pepper, spring onions, mushrooms and water chestnuts to the pan. Fry over moderately high heat, stirring frequently, until the vegetables are almost tender but still crisp.

Meanwhile, combine the soy sauce, sherry, stem ginger, cayenne and cornflour, stirring well.

Return the meat to the pan and fry for a further 1-2 minutes, stirring constantly.

Add the soy sauce mixture and stir to coat the meat and vegetables. Stir-fry for a further 1 minute. Serve this dish with saffron flavoured rice.

**Note:** Prepackaged stir-fry vegetables may be used in place of the celery, pepper, spring onions, mushrooms and water chestnuts.

# Raspberry orange delights

**SERVES 6**

*1 packet raspberry jelly*
*15 g (½ oz) sachet powdered*
  *gelatine*
*150 ml (¼ pint) boiling water*
*150 ml (¼ pint) cold water*
*190 g (6.7 oz) can frozen orange*
  *juice concentrate, thawed*
*300 ml (½ pint) vanilla ice cream,*
  *softened*

**To decorate:**
*orange slices*
*raspberries, fresh, frozen or canned*

Place the raspberry jelly and gelatine in a mixing bowl. Add the boiling water and stir until the jelly has melted and the gelatine dissolved. Stir in the cold water.

Strain the jelly mixture into a blender or food processor and add the orange juice (undiluted). Blend until smooth. Add the ice cream and blend again until smooth.

Pour the mixture into 6 dariole moulds. Chill until set.

To serve, dip the bottom of the moulds briefly in hot water, then turn out onto individual serving plates. Decorate with orange slices and raspberries.

*Variation:* Replace the raspberry jelly with strawberry or orange flavoured jelly and decorate with the appropriate fruit. Use flavoured ice-cream such as raspberry or strawberry ripple instead of vanilla.

● **Below left: Stir-fried pork with vegetables**
**Below right: Raspberry orange delights**

# INDEX

*Note:* this index includes variations to recipes and recipe tips